IMAGES
of America

CLEVELAND
POLICE

"I do solemnly swear that I will support the Constitution of the United States, the Constitution and laws of the State of Ohio, the Charter and ordinances of the City of Cleveland: obey the rules, regulations, and orders of the Division of Police of the City of Cleveland and will discharge the duties of my office to the best of my knowledge and ability, so help me God."

IMAGES
of America

CLEVELAND
POLICE

Cleveland Police Historical Society

ARCADIA

Copyright ©2005 by Cleveland Police Historical Society, Inc.
ISBN 0-7385-3370-X

Published by Arcadia Publishing
Charleston SC, Chicago IL, Portsmouth NH, San Francisco CA

Printed in Great Britain

Library of Congress Catalog Card Number: 2004115816

For all general information contact Arcadia Publishing at:
Telephone 843-853-2070
Fax 843-853-0044
E-mail sales@arcadiapublishing.com
For customer service and orders:
Toll-Free 1-888-313-2665

Visit us on the internet at http://www.arcadiapublishing.com

"The Poor Policeman" is the title of this c. 1900 photograph taken by well-known Cleveland photographer L. Van Oeyen.

(cover) Cleveland's safety director, Eliot Ness, poses with members of the Traffic Unit in 1938.

CONTENTS

FOREWORD

The history of the Cleveland Division of Police begins with the establishment of the marshal system in 1836, the same year as the incorporation of the great City of Cleveland. In 1859, the first Central Police Station was built. In 1867, we blazed a trail with the first use of mug shots. In 1900, the Murphy call box was designed and implemented first here in Cleveland. In 1911, one of the country's earliest mounted units was established. In 1917, we had the first ever conviction based on a palm print. The year 1936 brought the dawn of the Eliot Ness era. In 1957, for the first time anywhere, a bank camera took pictures of an unfolding bank robbery leading to the arrest and conviction of the robbers.

It is my sincere hope that as we look upon the pictures of the past, we see visions of what is yet to come. I know in my heart that our current generation of Cleveland police officers is at least the equal of our forebears and that our generation too shall leave as lasting a legacy as those whose footsteps we follow.

—Edward F. Lohn
Chief of Police, 2002–2005

INTRODUCTION

It is with feelings of pride hard to explain that the author presents this work to the people of Cleveland. And well might this be so. From the very outset, the utmost difficulty was experienced in obtaining data for the volume. Old police officers who have served on the force for more than three decades, the only persons directly connected with the workings of the department to whom one would naturally look for information, maintain a reticence only natural to men whose simple modesty is one of their many qualifications as a good officer.

Then, too, the older residents of the city, upon whom the writer was compelled to fall back, gave only disconnected stories in reference to the evolution of the department from the old city marshals to its present complete condition.

Owing to these facts, it became necessary to take the records from the old city journals, a patience-trying, arduous task. This became accentuated when it was found that several of the old journals were missing. The writer has been able, however, to give a complete record of the department from its very infancy when Marshal Kirk, in addition to his duties as a police officer, served in the capacity of city tax collector, down to the present writing, when the force is second to none and is looked upon with envy and respect by the other departments of the country.

The transformation from a little village six miles north of Newburgh Township to a city of the first grade and the ninth in size in the country makes an interesting tale. In relating this, I only tell the police end of it, but it will be noticed that the growth of the police department has been identical with that of the city and chronicles many of the important events that have been a part of the city's growth.

In looking over the 62 years of police history, one finds that there have been three epochs in its growth: its primary organization and ante-bellum marshals, the metropolitan police, the present system.

Histories galore, painting in variegated colors the events of the last century in regard to Cleveland, have made their appearance from time to time. But this volume will have the distinction of being the first record of any kind relating to the history of the police of Cleveland. In consequence, the writer asserts with confidence that this work will be largely read, and of a necessity, prove a valuable addition to the historical works of Cleveland.

In chronicling the events set forth in the history, the writer surely has nothing for which to apologize, the following pages, showing for themselves in plain black and white just what kind of a department the Cleveland Police Department is.

—Thomas A. Knight
September 1, 1898
(From the first published history of the Cleveland Police Department.)

A group of Cleveland Police officers poses for the camera, c. 1870.

One

CONSTABLES, MARSHALS, AND POLICEMEN

The history of the Cleveland Police Department is rooted in the history of the city. The origin of the department can be set at the exact moment Moses Cleaveland stepped onto the bank of the Cuyahoga River on July 22, 1796. According to William Ganson Rose, in his book *Cleveland: The Making of a City*, Moses Cleaveland was not only charged with conducting a survey of the future city that would bear his name but was authorized "to establish peace, quiet, and safety" in the new settlement. This directive, in effect, serves to clearly establish the city's founder as its first official peace officer.

The importance placed on maintaining law and order in the new settlement is further demonstrated by the fact that Lorenzo Carter, the man recognized as the area's first permanent settler, and Stephen Gilbert were appointed the township's first constables. The constables were responsible for policing a territory comprising 2,300 square miles. Their duties included census taking, murder investigations, and everything in between. Justice was carried out from a courthouse and jail built on the northwest corner of the public square. Public executions (hangings) were held there as well.

In 1830, Justice of the Peace George Hoadley "decided over twenty thousand cases, with few being appealed and none reversed." By 1836, "a wave of lawlessness and crime" caused the city to establish a "city watch," consisting of eight volunteer companies of six men each, which patrolled the city from sundown to sunup. Later that year, Cleveland was incorporated as a city, and an elected marshal was put in charge of the city watch.

In 1853, Watchman John Osborne became Cleveland's first law enforcement officer to die in the line of duty when a "miserable drunkard" stabbed him to death. In the ensuing years, over 100 more Cleveland police officers have given their lives protecting their city.

In the late 1850s and early 1860s, a movement began in the eastern United States to establish metropolitan police departments. In Cleveland, a watchman named Jacob W. Schmitt pushed the idea, and on May 1, 1866, the Cleveland Police Department was officially created. Schmitt would eventually become the longest serving police chief in the city's history. When Schmitt retired in 1893, the Cleveland Police Department had few peers and was recognized worldwide as model law enforcement agency.

At the turn of the 20th century, the Cleveland Police Department was developing innovative technology in the fields of criminal identification, adopting the Bertillion system and fingerprinting, and in communications with the design of a compact telephone and telegraph system that connected police officers on the street with precinct houses. Visitors from law enforcement agencies around the world came to see what was being achieved in Cleveland.

Chief Jacob W. Schmidt was instrumental in converting the antiquated and inefficient marshal's system of policing into an organized modern metropolitan police department. Chief Schmidt was the longest serving chief in the history of the department. With the exception of a gap of a few years, Schmidt was chief from 1866 until his retirement on June 19, 1893.

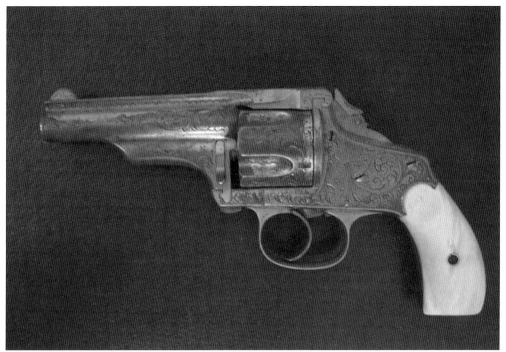

Pictured here is Chief Schmidtt's Merwin Hulbert Company .32 caliber revolver, customized with extensive etchings, a gold plated cylinder, and pearl handles.

Chief Schmidtt's badge is seen here.

Patrolman Michael Kick #42, a Civil War veteran, was shot and killed on the evening of June 14, 1875, near the intersection of Franklin Boulevard and Kentucky Street (West 38th Street) in a gun battle with members of the Blinky Morgan gang. He was the second city law enforcement officer to die in the line of duty. The first, Watchman John Osborne, a member of the City Marshal's Office, was stabbed to death on December 1, 1853.

Taken behind the police headquarters on Champlain Street, this 1875 photograph depicts what is believed to be the entire Cleveland Police Department. Chief Jacob Schmidtt is in the front row near the center.

Charles "Blinky" Morgan, aka "The Dude," was photographed in the Cleveland City Jail on July 2, 1887. Morgan and members of his gang were responsible for the murder of several police officers, including two from Cleveland, and wreaking havoc in Cleveland and throughout the Midwest for almost 20 years. His career ended at the end of a rope at the Ohio penitentiary, August 3, 1888.

PAT. HANLEY.   MATTHEW KENNEDY.   CHAS. MORGAN.   BILLY HARRINGTON.

$16,000.00 REWARD!

An enormous reward (for the time) was offered for these four members of the Blinky Morgan Gang, who were responsible for the deaths of Patrolman Michael Kick and Det. William Hulligan.

Members of the Cleveland Police Department depicted in this 1878 photograph are: (top row) Mather Ostermeyer #11, Charley Miller #116, A. W. Blood #87, John Burns #72, Wenzel Havlicek #29, John Williams #30, Daniel Cantillon #7, and James Waite #110; (middle row) "Dietz" (?), James Edwards #91, Jacob Schumacher #106, Charles Tressel #70, A. J. Marx #6, Cyrus Thomas #15, Theodore Keegan #47, Henry Seibel #97, and Edward Bradley #78; (front row) Jacob Ganks #46, Jacob Reese #83, Frederick Lambert #99, Charles M. McHannan #63, Henry Hoehn #32, John Shriber #66, John Bashold #124, and William Mylecraine #23.

Patrolman Frank Wagner was appointed June 23, 1869, and retired as a lieutenant on July 1, 1894.

The Cleveland Police Department's first permanent headquarters built on Champlain Street (currently the site of the Terminal Tower) is pictured here. The Central Police Station was built in 1861–1862.

Patrolman William M. Tucker #45 is believed to be the first black officer appointed to the department on June 3, 1881. Patrolman Tucker worked one of the downtown beats out of Central Station and retired on June 8, 1903.

Patrolman Charles S. Smith #6 was appointed January 28, 1897. He retired May 15, 1932, after achieving the rank of detective in 1918 and being promoted to secretary of police in 1922.

In 1890, this "open" patrol wagon, "the first black and white" (the modern nickname for a police patrol car), was assigned to the Second Precinct, located at the corner of Oregon and Oliver Streets (now Rockwell Avenue and East 24th Street). Patrolman Charles Schroeder is seated in the right rear.

Patrolman Joseph Mitschke #536, second from the left, is seen here c. 1907 with a group of his fellow officers and a "closed" patrol wagon, used for hauling arrestees to jail and conveying the sick and injured to the hospital.

Lydia Debere, aka "Cassie Chadwick," achieved world renown for perpetrating one of the biggest fraud cases in American history when she claimed to be the illegitimate daughter of industrialist Andrew Carnegie.

Form 11

OHIO STATE PENITENTIARY, No. 21978

Bertillon Measurements		
Height.	Head Length	L. Foot
1 M 67.0	18.4	22.4
Eng Ht	Head Width	L M F
5-5 3/4	15.1	10.9
Outer Arms	Cheek Width	L L F
1 M 67.8	13.5	8.2
Trunk 84.5	R Ear 6.3	L Fore A 43.7

Name Lydia De bere
Alias Cassie Chadwick
Crime Forgery
County Lucas Sentence 9 1/2 Year
Age 23 Weight 150 Build M. Stout
Hair M. Chest Complexion Fair
Born On Ocean Eyes M. Chest.
Occupation none
Received Jan. 23rd 1890 Discharged

Known or Admitted Former Imprisonment

MARKS, SCARS AND MOLES

This is Lydia Debere's booking card from the Ohio State Penitentiary (reverse side).

These Cleveland Police officers display their weapons, which were normally concealed in a pocket holster.

These Cleveland Police officers were photographed behind the old Central Police Station, c. 1887.

These officers are lined up in front of the nearly finished Champlain Street headquarters. The unidentified officer in the front row with the nightstick on his shoulder had one of the finest beards in the department. The fourth man in the front row is Lieut. John Dunn, who later became safety director under Mayor Tom L. Johnson.

The early 1900s Central Police Station was located at the corner of Champlain Street and Long Street and was demolished in the mid-1920s to make way for the construction of Cleveland Union Station—more commonly known as the Terminal Tower Complex.

In 1897, these plain-clothes officers posed in front of the Central Station on Champlain Street. Chief Corner is seated on the right.

Members of the Cleveland Police Department pose in front of the Central Station, *c.* 1920. The four women seated in the first row are police matrons whose duties pertained to the care of female prisoners. Matrons were first assigned to the department in 1893.

Two

THE DAWN OF
A NEW ERA

Cleveland began the 20th century as a city on the rise. Mayor Tom L. Johnson was elected to his first of four terms, and Cleveland, then the nation's sixth largest metropolis, was proclaimed to be the best governed city in America. Frederick Kohler was appointed chief of police and would be singled out by Pres. Theodore Roosevelt as "the best chief of police in America."

In those days, the department consisted of 350 officers, who were responsible for policing a population of 381,768—one third of which was foreign born. These officers worked out of seven precinct stations and patrolled 318 miles of roads. A rookie policeman worked 11-hour days and earned $65 per month. The question of how to spend his time off seldom arose, since there was so little of it. He was permitted one day off every 30 days.

Inspector Timothy J. Costello recalled, "If a policeman ever got licked while making an arrest or merely walking his rounds, he was in trouble. He could expect a beating at least once daily from then on." On the other hand, in order to answer the complaint that there was "never a policeman around when you needed one," 17 of the department's oldest, most experienced and valued officers were detailed to the busiest intersections in the downtown area to serve as walking information bureaus.

In 1903, the "sparrow patrol," a nickname for the Cleveland Police Department's bicycle squad, was formed to deal with the rapid rise of traffic related problems. Clevelanders owned more automobiles, per capita, than any other city in the world, and most of them were made in Cleveland. The department's annual report for that year counted 1,200 automobiles in the city. The Roaring '20s proved to be the most violent era in the city's history, and the most deadly for the police department. Between 1920 and 1930, no fewer than 19 Cleveland Police officers were killed in the line of duty.

In 1924, the department established a Women's Bureau, whose members were assigned to deal with all cases in which women or children were involved, either as victims or offenders. The women did not carry guns, nor did they wear uniforms, as it was thought this would hinder their effectiveness as investigators.

On January 13, 1931, George Matowitz was appointed chief of police, a post he would hold for over 20 years. Chief Matowitz died in office on November 29, 1951.

The officers in this *c.* 1910 photograph handled early traffic enforcement.

The department's first venture into the use of automobiles for police work was this 1911 White Motors Police Patrol Wagon, seen here parked behind the station's hitching post.

Chief Fred Kohler established the Cleveland Police Mounted Unit in 1911.

The officers assigned to the Haymarket Precinct around 1911 are seen here. The motorcycle

officers are mounted on Harley-Davidsons.

This is the first Cleveland Police Museum, *c.* 1900. "A Collection of Weapons Employed by Cleveland Murderers," an article found in a scrapbook compiled by George Laubscher from 1894–1906, described a "cabinet of horrors in city hall" where it stored "thousands of evidence from crimes." The cabinet is referred to as "a museum which has never been properly appreciated: few people know about it and fewer have visited it whereas under favorable conditions were it well managed it might have potential to be one of the strongest attractions in the city."

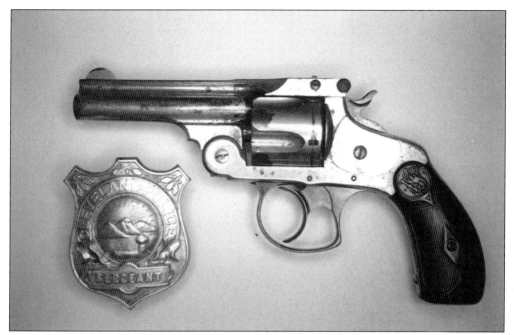

Smith & Wesson replaced Merwin Hulbert as the supplier of CPD handguns in the late 1800s. This S&W .38 caliber, double action revolver was shipped to the George Worthington Co. on March 7, 1891, for purchase by the Cleveland Police Department. The backstraps of these guns were engraved with the rank or badge number of the officer to which they were assigned (e.g. "C.P.D. Sergeant, #106 C.P.D.").

Patrolman John E. Gallagher #160 was appointed July 17, 1888, promoted to sergeant on December 15, 1900, and pensioned on May 8, 1918.

In August of 1910, Chief Fred Kohler shared the rear platform of President Theodore Roosevelt's train when the former president was in town to promote his new "Bull Moose Party."

Mayor Tom Johnson and Chief Frederick Kohler perform their annual inspection of the police department near East 6th and Superior Avenue in 1905.

Frederick Kohler, appointed July 16, 1889, became the chief on May 1, 1903, and was called the "best police chief in the United States" by Pres. Theodore Roosevelt. He was dismissed on March 17, 1913.

Pictured here are, left to right, Superintendent of the Bureau of Criminal Identification George Koestle, Inspector William S. Rowe, Chief of Police Fred Kohler, and newspaper reporter Bob Larkin on October 3, 1904.

On February 8, 1887, Det. William Hulligan, seated second from the left, was transporting a prisoner back to Cleveland from Pittsburg on the train when he was beaten to death by members of the Blinky Morgan gang, who were attempting to free their fellow gang member.

Patrolman Timothy Costello #326 (left) was the longest serving member of the Cleveland Police Department, having served for 57 years on active duty. Appointed on March 7, 1903, he died February 10, 1960, while still on the job and holding the rank of inspector. Patrolman Daniel J. O'Brien #243 (right) was appointed to the Cleveland Police Department on March 7, 1903, was pensioned as a captain June 13, 1957, after 54 years of service.

The two longest serving members of the Cleveland Police Department, Inspector Timothy Costello and Capt. Daniel O'Brien got together for this photograph about 1955.

The Motorcycle Unit, *c.* 1920, proudly display their Indian motorcycles.

On July 1, 1887, the Police Patrol and Exchange program began, largely through the efforts of former Western Union Lineman Jerry Murphy. He was responsible for the design of the now famous "Murphy Box." Each box contained a code-signal device and a telephone connected to the exchange. Every officer was issued an access key, inscribed with his badge number.

The Police Telephone Exchange at the Champlain Street headquarters is pictured here on April 28, 1926.

This group of Cleveland Police Officers is posing with their 1921 Peerless patrol car. The officer second from the right can be identified as the driver because of the gauntlets he is wearing.

"Black Maria," a 1915 Cleveland-built White Motors three-quarter-ton Police Emergency Patrol Wagon was used for conveying the sick and injured to the hospital and criminals to jail.

One of the original members of the Cleveland Mounted Police, Patrolman Jim Matowitz, who later commanded the unit, is seen here on Ontario Street, *c.* 1912.

Capt. Timothy Costello is "front and center" in this early Mounted Unit photograph, *c.* 1918.

Motorcycles became a part of the Cleveland Police Department inventory in 1911. This unidentified officer is riding an Indian, *c.* 1920s.

Patrolmen Robert O'Neill #595 and Julius Gleine #673 are seen at the Mounted Unit with some of the unit's traditional mascots.

The lonely job of the neighborhood beat man can be seen in this photograph taken *c.* 1915.

In the 1920s, patrol cars were still a relatively new concept, and these officers took the time to pose proudly with their mid-1920s Cleveland-built Peerless.

Patrolman Joseph Mitchke #536, appointed February 20, 1907, poses with an unknown partner about 1922.

The Cleveland Police Department's Band is pictured here in August 1919, when Cleveland

bragged of being the "Fifth City."

Chief of Police Jacob Graul meets with members his command on August 15, 1927. From left to right are the following: unidentified, unidentified captain, Deputy Inspector James Veasey, Capt. George A. Kadel, Inspector George Matowitz, Chief Graul, Inspector Martin A. Blecke, Inspector Cornelious Cody, Chief of the Women's Bureau Dorothy D. Henry, Superintendant of the Criminal Identification Bureau George Koestle, Deputy Inspector Martin J. Horrigan, and Deputy Inspector James J. Hughes.

This Cleveland Police Headquarters building, located between East 19th Street and East 21st Street on Payne Avenue, replaced the old Champlain Street headquarters that had to be torn down to make way for the Terminal Tower project. It served as police headquarters from 1925 until 1977, when the Justice Center was completed. The building still serves as Third District Headquarters and headquarters for the Bureau of Communication.

Here is a close-up of the infamous traffic control tower that was located for a brief period at the intersection of East 9th Street and Euclid Avenue in the late 1920s.

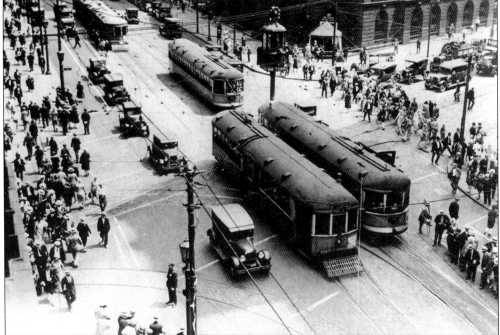

A police officer was posted in the cupola to observe traffic and could control the traffic signals several blocks in each direction. After it was struck several times by distracted drivers, the tower was removed.

A police officer uses a traffic semaphore to direct traffic on Public Square around 1920.

Police officers, as well as postmen, including Patrolman Robert A. Kern #560, adhered to the "neither rain, nor snow . . . " slogan, c. 1920.

Located at Broadway Avenue and Jones Street, the Seventh Precinct station was built in 1900–1901. This photograph dates to about 1920.

On May 15, 1929, a fire at the Cleveland Clinic had members of the Cleveland Police Department helping rescue patients and staff. The fire took the lives of 124 people and injured 92 more—including Cleveland Police Officer Otto Zizka #475, who eventually succumbed from poisonous smoke inhalation several years after the fire.

These prisoners were being unloaded from the "paddy wagon" and led into the station around 1925.

Sergt. Frank Milota Sr. and his son Patrolman Frank Milota Jr. track down trespassers by any means necessary in this photograph, *c.* 1930.

Sergt. Peter Mock (right) and his office crew prepare to meet visitors at their station house.

Working the Public Square beat, this patrolman helps to insure pedestrian safety.

The First Precinct Traffic Unit, around 1932, consisted of the following, from left to right: George Swansinger #985, three unidentified, George Stech #861 of the East 9th and Prospect beat, Joe Karl #704 of the Rockwell and East 9th Street beat, Charles Stipek #718, Andrew Bessick #231 of the East 6th and Superior Avenue beat, unidentified, and Joe Suchan #686 of the Public Square beat.

Three

NEW-ERA POLICING

On December 7, 1938, the Cleveland Police Department completely broke with the old method of policing that by then included 16 precinct station houses where the familiar neighborhood "beatman" was the backbone of the department. Instead, these officers were placed into radio-equipped "zone cars." The increasing popularity of the automobile made this change inevitable.

The department realized that the inter-state and inter-city crime problems and traffic flows of 1938 were very different from the past. Crime ceased to be a local problem. Criminals could reside in one city and steal their livelihood in another, distant, city. The beatman could no longer know when a man would leave his residence in an automobile, whether he was going to the bank to work or to rob it.

The police radio has become an extremely effective tool. In 1938, Cleveland Police Department vehicles had at their disposal 15 two-way radio frequencies. Previously, they had but one, and not too long before that radio receivers only.

The local precinct houses had become a handicap. Each precinct was manned by an administrative and operative staff and housed a number of reserves. Beatmen were required to be in the station a half hour to an hour out of each shift for roll calls and bulletins of the day. Two-way radios in the cars allowed this information to be broadcast directly to the cars. The remaining stations had all been equipped with teletype machines that made nine copies of each transmittal, so patrolmen no longer had to make hand-written notes. Shifts changes now occurred in the streets.

In place of the 16 old precinct stations, the city was divided into 32 zones. A specific number of zones made up a district, of which there were initially five, and a captain commanded each district. A zone car containing a sergeant and two patrolmen was assigned to each zone. Every fourth car had a lieutenant and two patrolmen. When each car reached its zone at the beginning of the shift, the central radio desk was notified, and a light on a map at headquarters was switched on to indicate the presence of that car.

In addition to the 32 zone cars, there were eight unmarked detective cars containing three men each. The Traffic Unit manned 35 two-man cars and up to an additional 17 accident prevention cars.

The assignment of three men to each car insured that the reserves would be available on the street rather than sitting idle in the stations. Officers were not expected to ride in the car for eight hours. Two men would get out and patrol on foot, while one would stay in the car to maintain contact with the radio. The driving job was rotated, so that all the men did sufficient footwork to keep in good physical condition.

Famous Chicago crime-buster Eliot Ness came to Cleveland after his stint in the "Windy City" and became Cleveland's safety director (1935–1941). He introduced many changes to the police department, including consolidating the 19 police precincts into 6 districts, improving training and taking officers off foot patrols and putting them in marked radio-equipped cars.

Safety Director Elliot Ness is seen here discussing his plan for the reorganization of the department, including the replacement of beatmen with mobile patrols, consolidating neighborhood precinct police stations into five police districts, and formalizing the training in the police academy.

Patrolman Frank W. Youngmann #134 participates in one of Safety Director Ness's traffic safety initiatives.

This edition of the *Cleveland Plain Dealer*, April 2, 1939, features an article about the "Torso Slayer" along with a map showing where the 12 victims' bodies were found and a photograph (top right) of the site where the 11th and 12th victims were discovered. The two photographs on the bottom left are of Detectives Martin Zalewski (top) and Peter Merylo (bottom), who had been working on the case for three years in an effort to find Cleveland's infamous murderer.

54

Det. Peter Merylo doggedly pursued the "Mad Butcher of Kingsbury Run" for years as a member of the Cleveland Police Department, and even followed leads after his retirement.

Det. Lloyd B. Trunk was in charge of the Bureau of Criminal Identification from 1935 through 1944. Detective Trunk made plaster death masks of the Torso Murderer's victims in hopes that they might be viewed and identified by members of the public.

A major part of the new safety director's plan to improve traffic safety in the city was the creation of the Accident Prevention Squad. The squad drove yellow Studebakers nicknamed "canary cars."

Until 1938, the Cleveland Police Department was limited to one-way radio communication with its police cars. This 1937 Chevrolet was one of the first cars equipped with a two-way radio.

The department replaced its old receiver-only radio system with a new fleet of zone cars all equipped with two-way radios in 1938. Patrolman Frank Dahlhausen #931 demonstrates the new equipment.

Pictured here is one of the new 1938 Ford "zone cars," all of which were equipped with new two-way radios and sported a red, white, and blue paint scheme.

This 1939 Harley-Davidson motorcycle was one of the first equipped with a radio receiver.

Patrolman Roy H. Wieland #1083 issues parking tickets while patrolling on his 3-wheel servi-car Indian motorcycle. Three-wheelers where chosen over two-wheeled bikes because of their superior handling during snowy Cleveland winters.

FBI Launches Cleveland

SCHOOL FOR "SUPER-POLICE"

Safety director from 1948 to 1952, Alvin J. Sutton, a former FBI man, set up a "graduate police school" using FBI agents to train veteran Cleveland Police Officers in the latest crime fighting techniques.

Capt. Mel J. Massey demonstrates the use of the Remington 12 gauge shotgun.

Patrolman James C. Burton #748 practices the proper shooting posture at the Grays Armory indoor range on September 28, 1949.

The 23rd cadet class poses with various weapons at the Cleveland Police Outdoor Range, *c.* 1946.

Although women could not become full-fledged police officers until the 1970s, they did prove their ability to handle weapons during training in the 1950s. Policewoman Barbara Yedlick Campbell #3003 demonstrated her proficiency with the Thompson sub-machine gun.

The November 18, 1941, edition of *Look Magazine* featured an article on Patrolman David Offut and his partner Patrolman Sam Zsvara. In four years, Offut, "Cleveland's No. 1 Amateur Stork," delivered 17 babies.

As part of the Cleveland Police Department's Traffic Safety Initiative, police officers worked closely with school crossing guards to insure the safety of children going to and from school.

In 1938, the "Finest Police Mounted Unit in the Land" parades down Euclid Avenue.

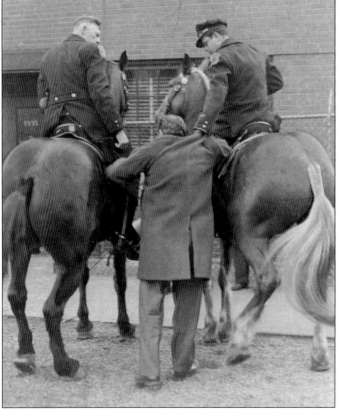

The Cleveland Mounted Police were often deployed to help control labor disputes that got out of hand. The police on horseback were especially effective in identifying agitators and separating them from the crowd. At this strike at the Anderson Company on March 18, 1947, Patrolman Robert A. "Pappy" Paisley assists in the removal of a strike agitator.

Chief George J. Matowitz (left) is seen here in this *c.* 1950 photograph. Appointed May 8, 1905, Matowitz (right) served as the city's police chief from October 16, 1930, until he died in office on November 29, 1951.

The department welcomed Chief Matowitz back after the civil service commission found no merit in charges brought against him by Mayor Burke. Matowitz would be the last chief to serve with civil service protection. Future chiefs would serve at the pleasure of the mayor.

The Fitzgeralds had a combined total of 105 years service on the Cleveland Police Department. Jim (left) served from 1938 until 1976, John (center) from 1934 to 1973, and Tom (right) served from 1942 until his death in 1971. The photograph dates from 1944.

Four

THE BUREAU OF CRIMINAL INVESTIGATION

The Cleveland Police Bureau of Criminal Investigation was established as the Cleveland Police Bureau of Criminal Identification in 1897 to deal more efficiently with the ever-increasing number of persons arrested each year. The department had become a model of efficiency, and Cleveland police officers were averaging more arrests per officer than their counterparts in other large cities.

Chief George Corner selected Patrolman George Koestle to head the new bureau because of his background as a commercial photographer. When the Criminal Identification Bureau began, an average of 40 prisoners a year were being photographed and measured in compliance with the Bertillion system of identification that had been developed in France.

The Bertillion system involved measuring specific body parts including foot size, hand size, size of the ears and nose, as well as recording the color of eyes and skin tone, moles, and other scars, marks, and tattoos. It was assumed that in measuring and recording these many distinct particulars relating to one individual, no other individual would have the exact same marks and measurements.

In 1904, Koestle persuaded Chief Fred Kohler to travel with him to the World's Fair in St. Louis to attend a convention of police chiefs. When they arrived, Koestle headed for the fingerprint exhibit being presented by detectives from England's Scotland Yard. Subsequently, Koestle was invited to attend the first fingerprint class ever held in the United States. Having become convinced that fingerprints were more reliable and easier to manage than the cumbersome Bertillion system, Koestle lobbied hard and eventually won approval to make fingerprinting the primary method of criminal identification in the Cleveland Police Department. Koestle was made a detective in 1906, and by the time he retired in 1939, the Bureau of Criminal Identification was photographing and fingerprinting more than 6000 persons each year. George Koestle was named "Dean of American Fingerprinting" for his 40-plus years of service in the field of criminal identification.

If science could crack the riddles of crime, then its wizard would have been David Cowles. A pioneer in the field of ballistics, he became one of the country's best-known forensic experts. Cowles started the department's polygraph program and established the Scientific Investigation Unit (SIU), becoming the unit's first superintendent. The SIU ultimately absorbed the Bureau of Criminal Identification, and with Cowles's leadership and innovation, continued to be known in law enforcement circles as one of the best in the world.

With over 40 years of service, SIU Superintendent Victor Kovacic continues the tradition of long-serving heads of this unit. Under his leadership, SIU has maintained a modern and efficient laboratory.

The Cleveland Police Department first began using photography as a means to identify the criminal element in the late 1860s. Initially, photographs were made at commercial portrait studios, sometimes posing the suspects in groups as a cost-cutting measure. CPD personnel began making their own photographs in 1898. This early "mug shot" (no. 35) of George Robertson is dated May 8, 1867.

Mug shot no. 206 depicts Albert W. Chamberlin, who murdered John McConcoughgey. Chamberlin died of cholera in the Ohio State Penitentiary in 1873.

The reverse of Florence Clark's (aka "Ora Starr") no. 5553 mug shot lists her as a "suspicious person" and includes descriptions of various physical characteristics in accordance with the Bertillion system of identification.

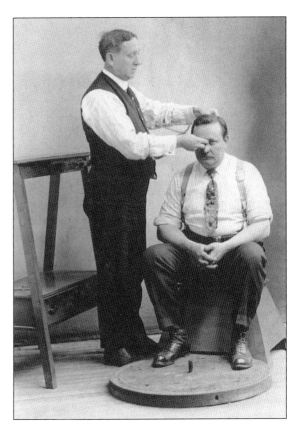

The basis of the Bertillion system of identification, developed in France in the age before fingerprinting, was a record of distinct body measurements, coloring, and markings. Here, Superintendent Koestle demonstrates Bertillion techniques to his "suspect," Det. Frank Texler.

The Cleveland Police Department was on the cutting edge of technology at the turn of the century, when the use of fingerprints as a means of identification was becoming an accepted tool for law enforcement. The officer with the badge in this picture is George Koestle, who would become known as the "Dean of American Fingerprinting." Koestle is instructing a group of detectives in the Champlain Street Headquarters around 1905.

One of the keys to using fingerprints as a law enforcement tool is organizing a good system. Fingerprints, even today, rely heavily on visual examination by a police officer to make the system work. This is the fingerprint file room at the old police headquarters, c. 1920.

George Koestle examines one of the thousands of fingerprints he had charge of over during his many years of service.

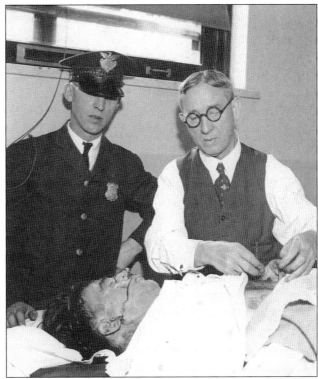

Superintendent of Criminalistics George Koestle obtains fingerprints from the body of a robbery suspect killed in a shootout with police.

David Cowles succeeded George Koestle as the Superintendent of Criminalistics and also became a nationally known leader in the field of science in law enforcement. By today's standards, the methods then in use were crude, but new inroads in the use of science and technology as tools for the police were constantly being made.

Superintendent David Cowles poses with a "death mask," which were plaster casts made from the corpse of an unidentified body as an aid to identification. Death masks sometimes had hair and makeup added in order to more closely resemble the unidentified person.

Victor Kovacic, who followed David Cowles as the superintendent of SIU, is seen here (left) securing a weapon found at a crime scene.

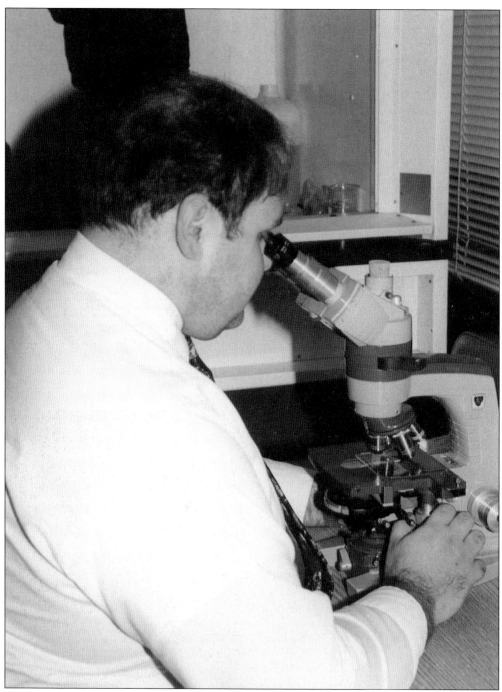

Trace evidence being examined by a SIU technician.

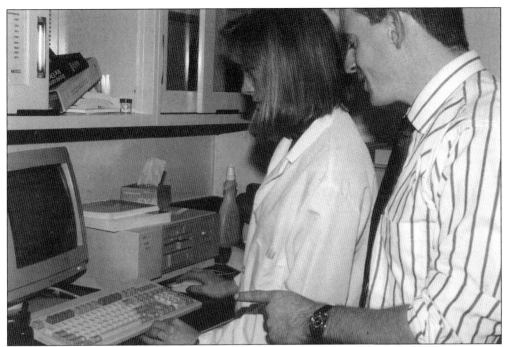

Thousands of pieces of evidence pass through the SIU Forensic Lab each year. Each item is closely monitored, and great care is taken to prevent contact and contamination with anything that may compromise its value.

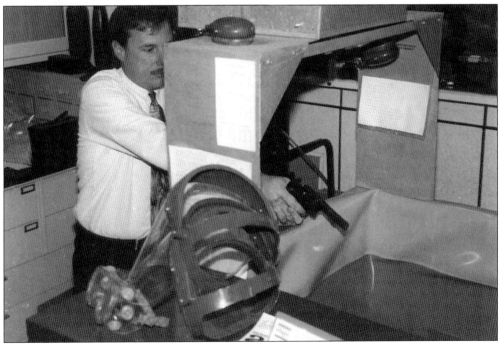

SIU Sergt. Dan Rowley test fires a handgun into a water-filled tank designed to trap the bullet, undamaged, so it can be examined.

The Cleveland Mounted Police made their first of several appearances in presidential inaugural parades during the second inauguration of President Dwight D. Eisenhower in January of 1956.

Five

THE MODERN CLEVELAND POLICE DEPARTMENT

The period of time between the early 1950s and early 1960s were among the most tranquil in the political history of Cleveland. Nevertheless, the police department continued to advance by developing new strategies to improve traffic safety and fight crime.

The death of Chief George Matowitz, the 13th chief in the department's history, represented the end of an era. Matowitz was one of a handful of survivors of the capable young men brought into the department during the reforms of Chief Fred Kohler at the turn of the 20th century. He would be the last chief of police to serve under civil service. Since his death in 1951, 25 others have served as chief, some for a matter of days.

During this time, the face of the city itself was changing as a result of urban renewal and construction of the interstate highway system. Long familiar neighborhoods vanished, and many of those that remained became unrecognizable.

Rioting broke out in the city's Hough neighborhood for six days in 1966, and for the first time since the violent labor strikes of the 1930s, the National Guard had to be called to maintain order. As bad as this situation was, it was only a prelude to the most tragic day in the department's history.

On the evening of July 23, 1968, the Glenville neighborhood exploded with violence. Police officers from every part of the city responded, and by night's end, three police officers had been killed and another would suffer, paralyzed, for 25 years before dying in 1993. Fourteen other police officers were injured, including 11 who had been shot. The rioting continued until the police and National Guard were able to restore order on July 28.

In the 1970s, policewomen and policemen became "patrol officers," as women were, for the first time, assigned to basic patrol along side their male counterparts. The department's motto "Our Men Serve All Men" was replaced with "Proud to Serve." Additionally, increased recruitment of minorities to the department made great strides in making the department more reflective of the racial make up of the city.

During this last part of the 20th century, the friction between the police and the city administration seemed always on the rise. There were police strikes, police lay-offs, and constant confrontations between the mayor's office and the police department.

The Cleveland Police Department entered the 21st century with hope and confidence. The Cleveland Police Department, which has played a major role in the development of this community, can look to itself with a deep sense of pride, having served a great city for more than 150 years.

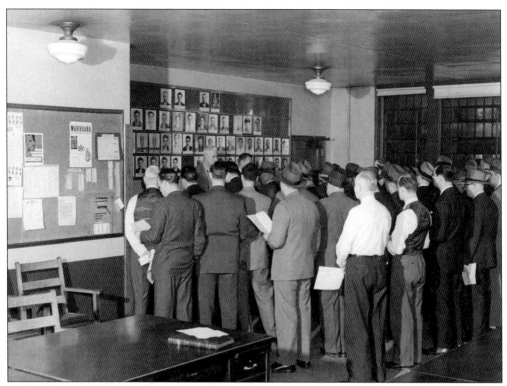

Detectives working out of the Central Station at East 21st and Payne Avenue held roll call on the building's third floor. Posted in the roll call room were photographs of wanted and suspected criminals, as well as other information—including a poster explaining how to detect marijuana.

The Bureau of Criminal Identification, located in the Central Station, was the central repository for photographs and fingerprints. Although now situated in Police Headquarters in the Justice Center, it continues to be the place victims can go to review "mug shots" in an attempt to identify suspects in crimes.

The evolution of the emergency patrol wagon is evident in this roomier and better-equipped Dodge, c. 1955. The wagons were used to haul prisoners to jail and convey the sick and injured to hospitals. Police officers trained in basic first aid continued this tradition until the inception of the Emergency Medical Service in the 1970s. You can still dial MAIN-1-1234 (621-1234) to reach the police operator.

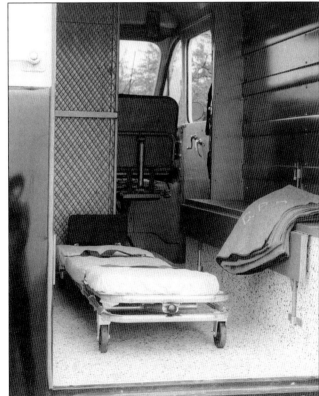

This collage of photographs from the mid-1950s was used to display the various functions of the police department.

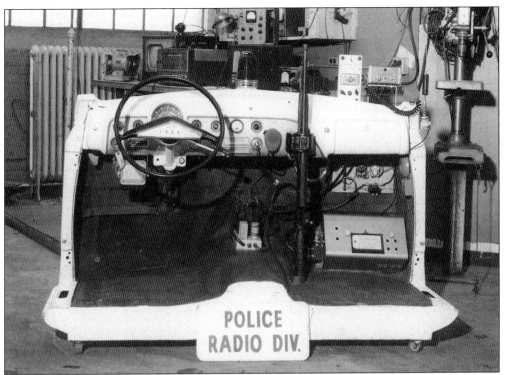

This mockup, c. 1955, was used to help the technicians figure out the best way to install the latest radio equipment into patrol cars.

Third District zone car 315, a 1956 Ford Police Interceptor, was equipped with a new and improved radio system, which included a "six-meter" whip antenna. Previously the antennae were hidden away under the car.

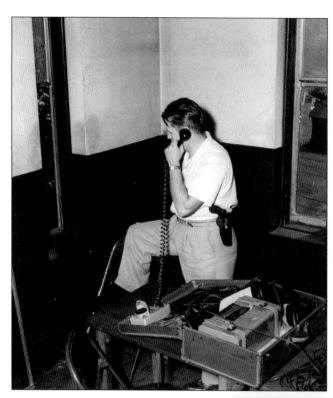

In an effort to keep crime in check, police everywhere employ the "stake out" to surveil and arrest criminals. In these photographs, *c.* 1956, the police officer in "the perch" keeps an eye on the street below, where numerous cars had been broken into.

The suspects were unaware they were being watched, photographed, and surrounded by undercover police officers.

Caught completely off guard, the suspects were placed in police custody moments after they made their break-in to the automobile.

This bank, now a Charter One Bank, at 6235 St. Clair Avenue, was the scene of the world's first bank robbery to be filmed by a bank security camera. The robbery occurred shortly after noon, April 12, 1957. Son of Police Chief Frank Story and superintendent of police communications, Thomas E. Story is displaying the camera.

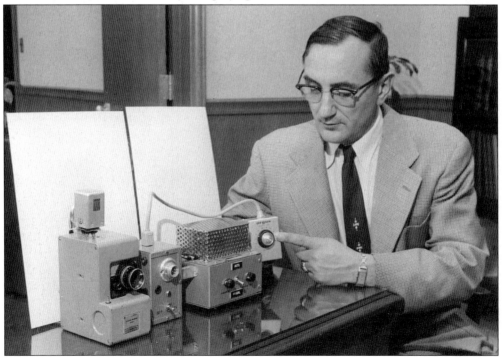

Later that same day, detectives reviewed films from the bank camera, identified the suspects, and broadcast the footage on the national news. By combining good detective work and the use of this new technology, the suspects were soon arrested.

The three robbery suspects, awaiting their arraignment with doom in their eyes, read of their demise at the hands of the Cleveland Police Department.

Although blurry, this frame from the actual film depicts the male suspect pointing his gun across the teller window where his accomplice, the woman in the dark coat, helps herself to the bank's money.

"No stick-up man in his right mind will walk into a bank with a hidden camera peering at him out of a wall" said Chief Frank Story, April 12, 1957. Proving this statement to be overly optimistic, a robber attempts to disable this camera by shooting at it, c. 1970.

In 1959, these women were training with firearms. They are under the watchful eye of Lieut. Michael Roth, far right. The police women, from left to right, are Ruby Scott, Ruth May, Patricia Cozens, Jean Aber, and Joanne Timkovic.

The Cleveland Police Department's Marching Unit prepares for the annual St. Patrick's Day Parade on March 17, 1962.

The Cleveland Police Department Mobile Communications bus could be used at remote sites and for large-scale special operations. It is pictured here around 1963.

On July 4, 1963, the communications bus was deployed for the Independence Day celebration. The staff included, left to right, Capt. Pete Becker, unknown, Patrolman Anton S. Lohn #93, Superintendent Tom Story, Katherine Sutkow, unknown, and Policewoman Susan Boyd #3006.

On October 31, 1963, Det. Martin McFadden, age 62 with 39 years on the job, confronted three men acting suspiciously in front of a downtown shop. The three men were detained by McFadden, and when he patted them down to check for weapons, he launched a case that went on to the Supreme Court of the United States as "Terry *v.* Ohio," which became a hallmark for every law enforcement officer since.

John Woodall Terry, a career criminal, and two accomplices were preparing to rob a downtown store when Detective McFadden confronted them. Even by the time this mug shot was made in 1956, Terry had the proverbial "rap sheet as long as your arm."

Sergt. Anthony Coyne, president of FOP Lodge number eight; Deputy Inspector Carl C. Bare, state FOP president; and Ralph A. Bonacci, CPD Tow Unit and president of FOPA no. 23; ensured that the public was aware of the first annual celebration of National Police Week and Peace Officers Memorial Day, as proclaimed by President John F. Kennedy in 1963.

Prior to the widespread use of suntan lotion, this member of the Cleveland Police Mounted Unit warns this young beachcomber to cover up.

Det. Robert F. Shankland prepares
for the use of tear gas at an
incident at East 19th Street and
Payne Avenue in 1964.

As a response to the Supreme
Courts ruling that all suspects
were to be advised of their
constitutional rights before any
questioning, the "Miranda
Warning" was posted at the
Fifth District booking window.
From left to right are Patrolman
James V. DiFranco #218,
Patrolman Casimir S. Roszak
#943, and Detective O'Donnell.

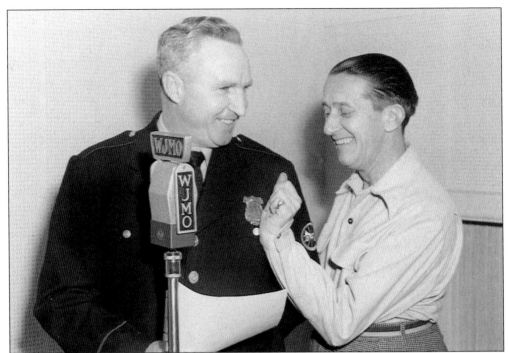

Local and national celebrities loved to work with the Cleveland Police Department, either under the protection of a security detail or on a public education/community relations campaign. Before he began his long-running television variety show, Gene Carroll was a broadcaster for WJMO-Radio. Here he is with Patrolman Patrick E. Cooney #289, c. 1949.

Ron Penfound, host of the *Captain Penny Show* (1955–1971), is seen here with Cleveland police officers including Patrolman William D. Schueneman #439, the motorcycle officer on the left.

Talk show host Mike Douglas helped promote a public relations campaign with Patrolman Elmer Goltz #511 and Patrolman Charles J. Brynak Jr. #1121.

National variety show host Ed Sullivan greets members of the Cleveland Police Mounted Unit, including Patrolman Arthur Lettieri #876, center.

Former Pres. Harry S Truman is pictured here in 1960 with (left to right) Patrolman Joseph A. Dura #1068, Patrolman Edward R. Misencik #776, Patrolman Leo Hayes #1249, and Sergt. Patrick Gallagher.

Cleveland Police Sergt. Anthony Nachtigal, president of the Fraternal Order of Police Lodge number eight, meets Pres. John F. Kennedy at Hopkins Airport during a presidential visit in October of 1962.

Cleveland Mayor Ralph Perk demonstrates his equestrian skill during a visit to the Cleveland Police Mounted Unit, *c.* 1973.

With the use of their mobile equipment trailer, members of the Cleveland Police Ports and Harbors Unit are able respond to water-related emergencies at inland lakes and streams and along the shoreline, where their larger patrol boats are unable to reach.

The *Lex* (Latin for "law") was designed by Cleveland Police Lieut. John "Jack" Delaney, the first officer in charge of the Ports and Harbors Unit. Launched in 1963, the *Lex*, which is still in service, was built by the Inland Seas Boat Company of Sandusky, Ohio.

The *Rookie* belies its name, as it was one of the unit's real workhorses allowing these police officers to get closer to the target when performing rescues and recoveries. Patrolman Richard E. Ryan #573 is at the oars.

The *Bluecoat*, obtained in 1964 and smaller and faster than the *Lex*, was an additional tool to be used by the Ports and Harbors Unit in their quest to make the water a safe place to enjoy.

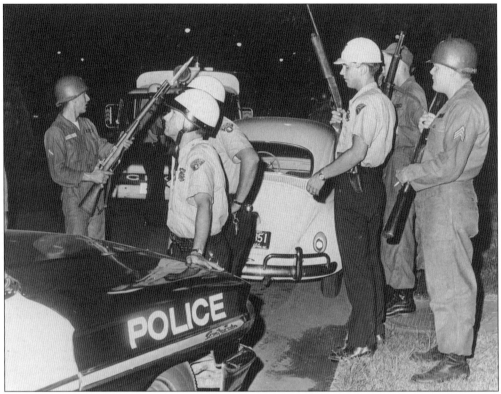

The Cleveland Police Department was put to its limit in the summer of 1966 when the Hough neighborhood erupted in violence. The Ohio National Guard was called in to help the department restore order.

The Hough riots drew national attention. Additional agitators prone to violence from outside of the city, as well as the curious, were drawn to the riot area.

In July of 1968, the Glenville neighborhood was turned into a battle zone that began when three police officers were killed in an ambush that eventually led to several days of rioting. These heavily armed police officers assemble for roll call at the Fifth District.

Police officers from throughout the city responded to the call for help when the rioting began.

Lieut. Leroy Jones (*left*), Patrolman Louis Golonka #1831 (*lower left*), and Patrolman Willard Wolff #1740 (*lower right*) all died of wounds received that day. Patrolman Thomas Smith #1232 died on March 9, 1993, after suffering the effects of his wounds for 25 years. Fourteen other Cleveland Police Officers were injured that day, including 11 that were shot.

In August of 1966, these two Cleveland Police Officers prepare to rush an apartment at 629 Eddy Road in search of a bank robber.

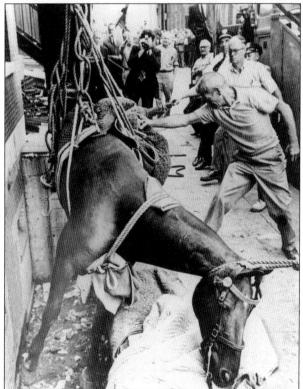

The hazards of patrolling an urban environment on horseback are many. Police horse "Tony" escaped from his tether and fell through a grate covering a window well on Euclid Avenue in 1969. The Mounted Unit veterinarian Dr. Dan Stearns (with glasses), Lieut. Ed Troyan, and Police Officer Carl Bultrowitz are evident in the background.

In a time before women were assigned to duty in zone cars, they wore these uniforms, as modeled by Elsie Bryant #437 and Elaine Newsome outside the Second District Headquarters on Fulton Avenue.

These women of the Cleveland Police Department are posing for the camera around 1967.

The officer on the left is Patrolman Edward Murray #507, a 32-year veteran of the Cleveland Police Department who was killed in the line of duty on July 2, 1975. Police Officer Murray is shown here with Safety Director McCormick, Police Officer John P. Gaughan #14, and Police Officer Edward P. Goggin #1506.

Capt. Jerome Poelking, the chief of detectives, presents retiring Det. Lee Peters his retirement plaque. Captain Poelking died in the line of duty in 1975. Standing behind Captain Poelking, in the plaid sport coat, is the future chief of police Edward Kovacic.

Members of the Cleveland Police Department are obligated to keep up their shooting skill and for years used the range at the historic Cleveland Gray's Armory on Bolivar Road for training.

This is what target practice looks like if you are the target.

In the 1970s, Cleveland police zone cars were painted "safety green" and bore the motto "Our Men Serve All Men." The color of the cars and the department's motto were both short lived.

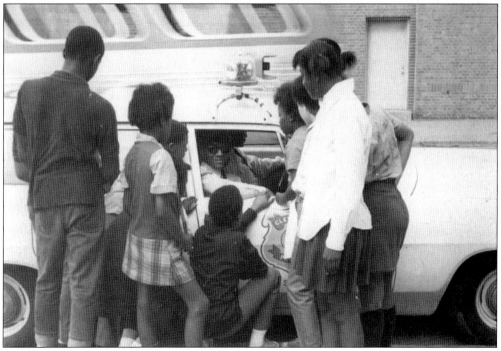

After the riots of the 1960s, the Cleveland Police Department made a strong effort to develop closer ties with the community they served as demonstrated by these officers "rapping" with some of the kids in their neighborhood.

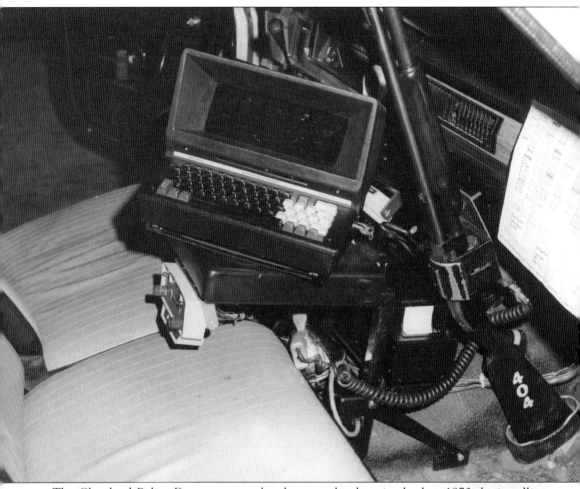

The Cleveland Police Department explored new technology in the late 1970s by installing computers in zone cars. The new computers were prone to numerous breakdowns and were not in use for long before it was realized that their dependability was not up to par. The piece of paper attached to the dashboard of the car is a "hot sheet"—a list of cars recently stolen in the city. Hot sheets are still used as a quick reference and back up to the computers now installed in all zone cars.

Although the Mounted Unit was always popular with the public, Patrol Officer Sam Reese #1712 performs one of the many functions suited to the mounted officer that is *not* necessarily popular.

Police Officer Michael Dugan #897 and Police Officer Jonathon McTier #1588 check crime clusters on a pin map at the Impact Task Force office in 1974.

The current Police Headquarters building was completed in 1973 as a component of the Justice Center complex in downtown Cleveland. The former headquarters building then became the Third District headquarters.

Patrol Officers Sharon Caine and
Valerie Jones belie the slogan
"Our Men Serve All Men."

Except for the Third District, the
Cleveland Police Department operates
jails in each one of its district stations,
as well as the Central Prison Unit in
the Justice Center. In the 1990s,
correctional officers, who are employees
of the police department, replaced
police officers assigned to the jails.

(*above*) "Mother" was the nickname of the SWAT Unit's armored communication and rescue vehicle. Over the years, this vehicle has been a welcome sight to anyone, police or civilian, threatened by a suspect's gunfire. Mother has been credited with saving dozens of lives and quelling many severely dangerous situations by its mere presence. In service since the early 1970s, Mother was recently retired and is now "assigned" to the Cleveland Police Historical Society.

(*left*) On January 4, 1985, a mentally ill female wounded a Hopkins Airport ticket agent and attempted to hijack a jetliner. Four hostages were held. The decision to attempt a rescue was made, and the CPD SWAT Team boarded the plane. The hijacker fired off a shot at one of the officers, who was saved by his body amour. The hijacker was wounded and incapacitated, and the hostages were rescued unharmed.

The *Jack F. Delaney*, named in honor of the founder of the Ports and Harbors Unit, was the finest police boat on the Great Lakes when it was launched in 1985.

Cleveland police officers often arrive on the scene of fires or other medical emergencies before the Fire Department or EMS. Here, uniformed and plain clothes officers attend to the victim of a shooting—giving first aid and comfort and at the same time obtaining valuable information and evidence relating to the circumstances of the incident.

The Cleveland Police Department finally patrolled the city by land, sea, and air when the Aviation Unit was activated on January 2, 1990, comprised of two Schweitzer 300C helicopters and six officers.

The "old ways" met the "new ways" in this manhunt for a criminal suspect.

Being a police officer in Cleveland is not all "down and dirty." Police Officer William Wagner #2542 and Police Officer Patrick Evans take time to do what being a police officer is all about, helping people.

For as long as anyone can remember, the Cleveland Police Department has maintained a holiday tradition of raising money to provide food baskets to needy families in their respective districts.

The Cleveland Police Department established a K-9 Unit in 1989 with dogs that specialized in bomb detection, tracking, drug detection, and general utility.

Police Officer Bob Patton #2469 and his partner Oden, working the downtown safety patrol beat.

At the beginning of each shift, officers attend roll call to insure that they all have the proper uniform and equipment; receive their daily assignment, and any special information that needs to be passed along—such as areas of special attention and recent crimes.

In the 1990s, sobriety checkpoints became a law enforcement fad as a tool to combat the drunken driving problem. Even today, if you approach a DUI checkpoint and see this image in this manner, you may be in trouble.

The Cleveland Police Traffic Unit operates this mobile police station to assist with the enforcement of the DUI laws. The Breath Alcohol Testing Mobile Unit, or "BAT Mobile," is equipped to test, book, and hold drivers suspected of alcohol related offenses.

This group of suspects has been placed under the control of this officer during the "bust" of a known drug house.

Law enforcement personnel, from the constables of the early 1800s and members of the city's night watch in the mid-19th century, to today's deputy marshals and police officers have patrolled the city streets on foot. Police Officer George Schultz #2243 and Police Officer Nicholas Moutsus #868 "walk the beat" in the Playhouse Square area.

Police Officer Don Williams #1222 and Police Officer Brian Fischer #1349 patrol the city's Third District.

In 1997, this armored rescue vehicle was purchased by the Cleveland Police Department to replace its ailing and aged predecessor. Known as "Mother II," it is deployed during high-risk situations—as well as community events, where the citizens of Cleveland warmly receive it.

During the 1990s, bicycles came back into use as a law enforcement tool after an absence nearly 75 years. The bicycle officer was seen as a community relations tool, removing officers from the insulation of the zone car and making them more accessible to the public.

The Cleveland Police Department Motorcycle Unit, part of the Bureau of Traffic, has been and continues to be an invaluable asset in the department's mission to insure traffic safety. With the use of a portable radar gun, these motorcycle officers are able to monitor the speed of approaching traffic.

The Cleveland Police Department operates a police station inside Hopkins International Airport. Prior to 9/11, officers assigned to the Hopkins Airport Unit provided security patrols, assisted with traffic control, and were available to travelers to handle reports of crimes, give directions, and answer questions. Their mission has taken on an entirely different tone in these post 9/11 days, when airport security has become a nationwide focus.

In the early 2000s, the Aviation Unit replaced their aging Schweitzers with two MD 500e helicopters equipped with half-million candlepower searchlights and FLIR (Forward Looking Infrared) for nighttime surveillance.

The Pipes and Drums of the Cleveland Police, established in 1996, is seen here during a St. Patrick's Day parade, c. 2000.

In the spirit of the holidays, and the desire to contribute to the community, a group of police officers led by Capt. Joseph Sadie (far right) created the Cops, Kids and Christmas program. They distributed toys and candy throughout the city during the Christmas season. The program was recently expanded, and the name changed to simply Cops and Kids, in order to reflect a now year-round effort to accomplish its goals.

Communications is possibly the most important tool in the modern police department's arsenal. The CPD Communications Unit recently moved into a modern, computer-aided dispatch center, which it shares with EMS and the fire department. Hundreds of thousands of calls for service are received and handled each year.

On October 30, 2002, after an absence of almost 25 years, 28 computers were installed in Fourth District zone cars that were participating in the "Mobile Data Terminal Computer Pilot Project." By 2004, all CPD zone cars were equipped with these mobile data terminals.

The department confiscated this corvette after it was used to facilitate a criminal enterprise. It was cleaned up, painted black and white, and equipped with police radios so it could be used as a traffic enforcement car and community relations tool.

The "badge case" in the lobby of the Justice Center holds the badges of 106 Cleveland Police Officers that have died in the line of duty. When a Cleveland police officer falls, his badge is retired—never to be issued again. It is displayed with honor to remind us all of his sacrifice.

This is a collage of officers of the Cleveland Police Department, *c.* 2001.

AFTERWORD

The Cleveland Police Historical Society is listed as the author of this book, but it is, of course, impossible for the society *per se* to author anything. Therefore our thanks go to those who contributed their time and effort to this project. Society Trustee Patrol Officer Thomas Armelli #618 was the principal writer and photograph editor. Collaborating with Officer Armelli on editing and image scanning was Cleveland Police Historical Society Executive Director David C. Holcombe. Staff members Allan Coates and Marilyn Jech also contributed.

Much of the text has been adapted from previously published CPHS works. For these sources, we gratefully acknowledge Thomas G. Matowitz Jr., T. S. Peric, and the late Thomas A. Knight.

CPHS Mission Statement

The Cleveland Police Historical Society exists to collect and preserve Cleveland's significant police history, and to use its collections and programs to interpret police history to foster mutual understanding and respect between law enforcement officers and the public. Please visit their website, http:\\www.clevelandpolicemuseum.org, for more information.